treble clef

1. E

2. G

3. B

4. D

5. F

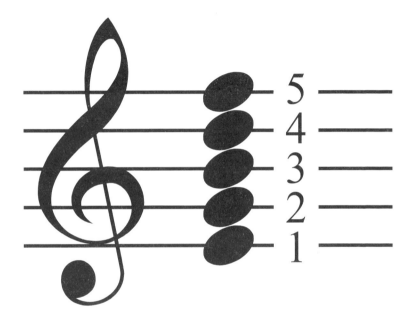

1. F

2. A

3. C

4. E

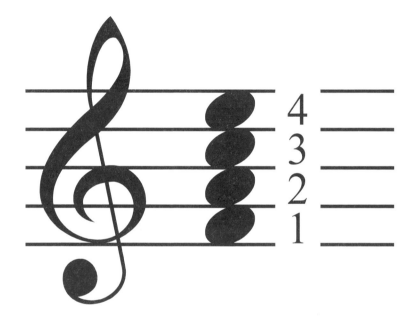

sharp

flat

whole
note

half
note

quarter note

eighth note

dotted note

triplets

whole
rest

half
rest

quarter rest

eighth rest

4/4 time

four beats per measure, quarter note gets one beat

$\frac{4}{4}$ or C

$\frac{3}{4}$ time

three beats per measure, quarter note gets one beat

3
4

6/8 time

six beats per measure, eighth note gets one beat

68

tie

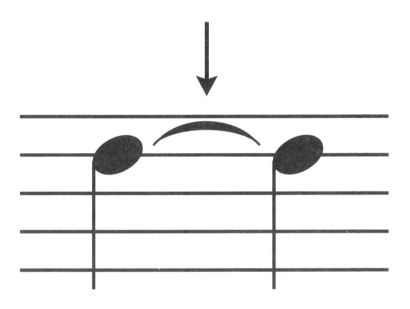

fermata

downstroke

upstroke

rate of
speed

Tempo

how loud or
soft to play

Dynamics

the distance between two pitches

Interval

repeat signs

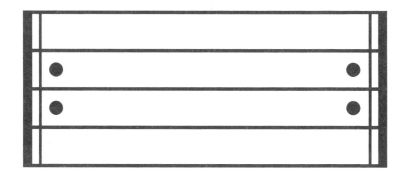

endings

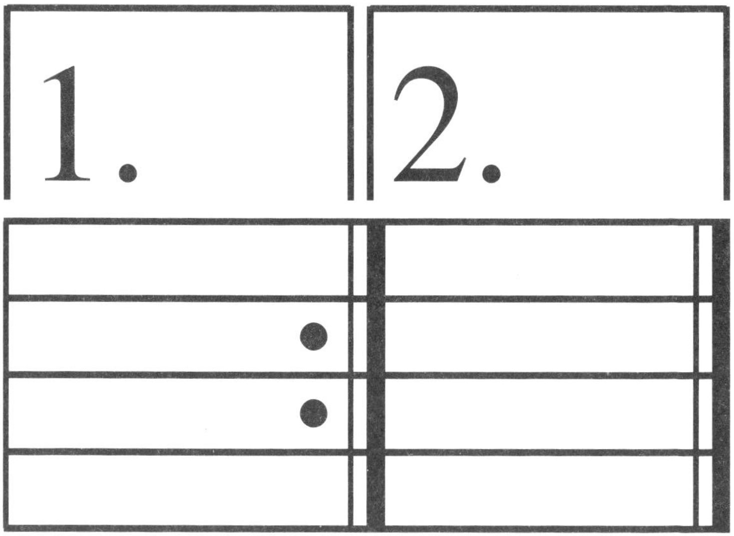
1.
2.

endings

27

Return to the beginning (capo) and play until the first coda sign ⊕ then skip to the next coda sign

D.C. al Coda

Return to the segno sign 𝄋 and play until the first coda sign ⊕ then skip to the next coda sign

D.S. al Coda

Return to the segno sign 𝄋 and play to the end (fine)

D.S. al Fine

E

F

F#

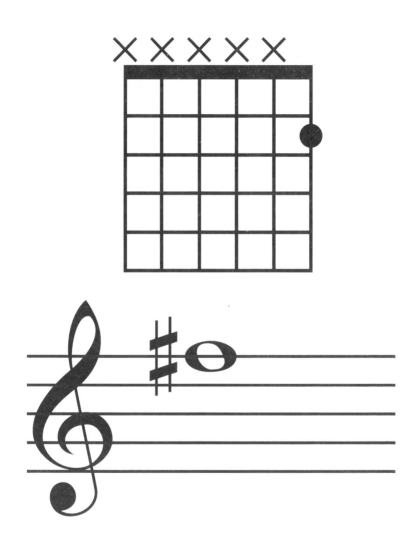

G

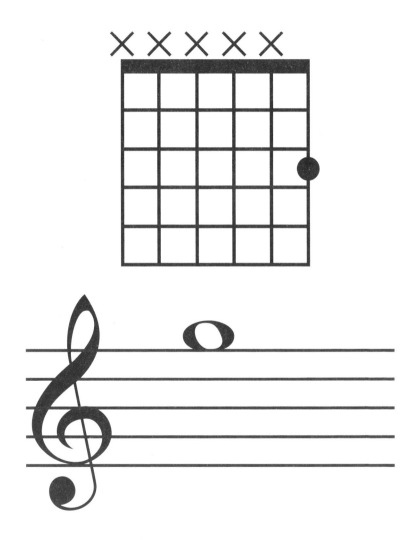

G#

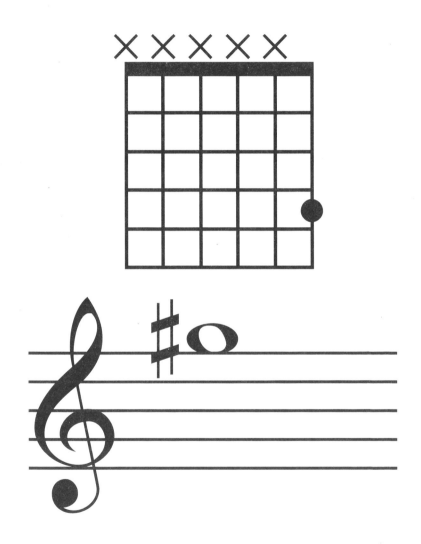

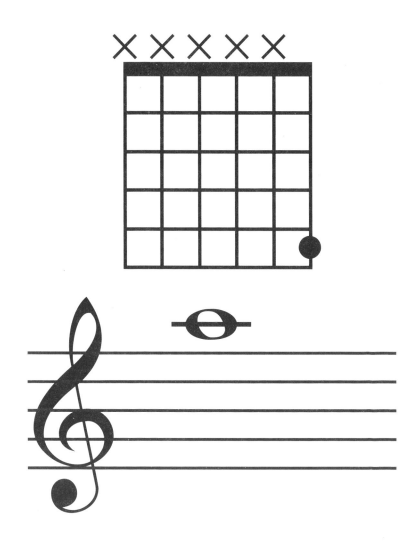

B

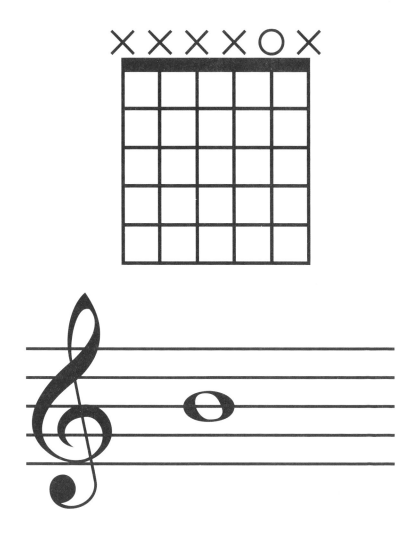

C

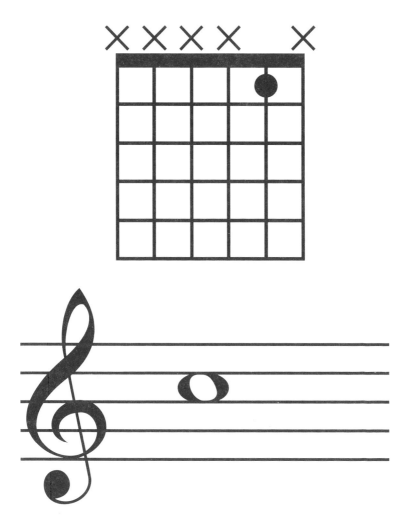

C#

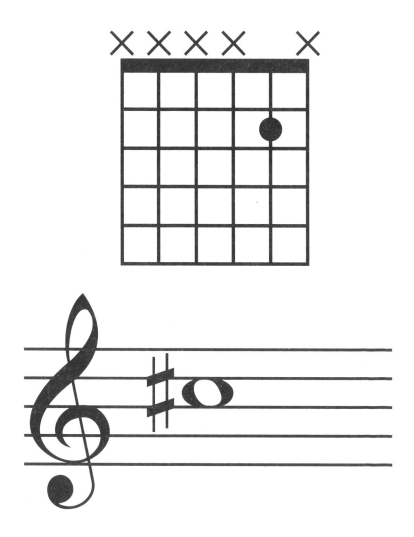

D

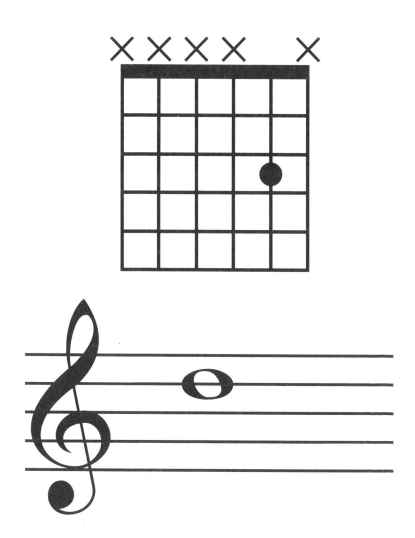

D♯

41

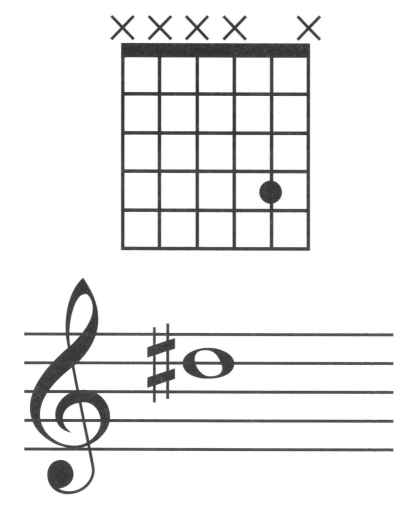

E

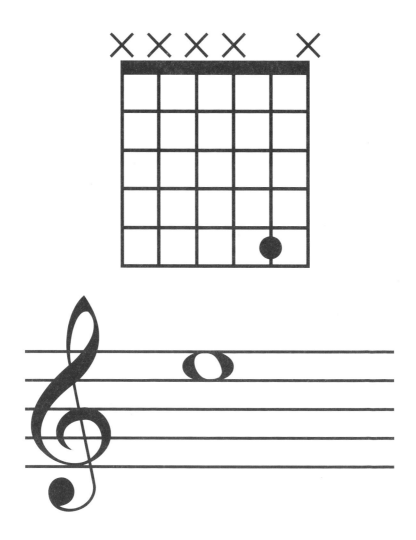

G

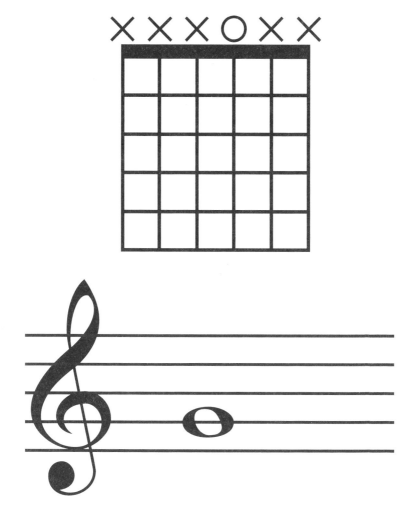

G#

A

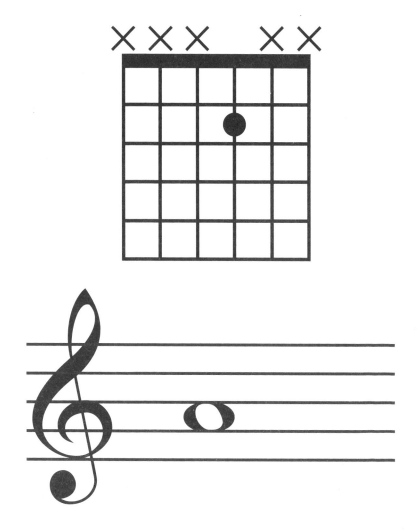

B♭

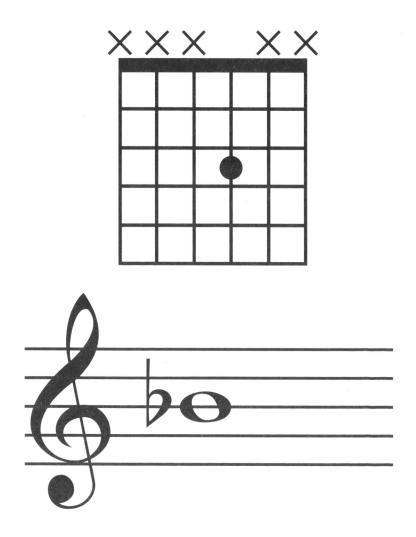

B

C

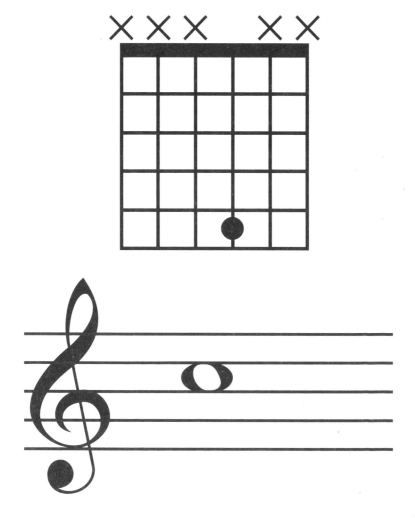

D

E♭

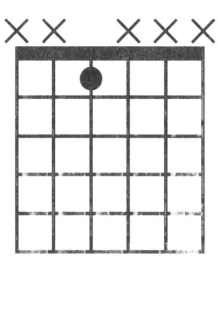

E

51

F

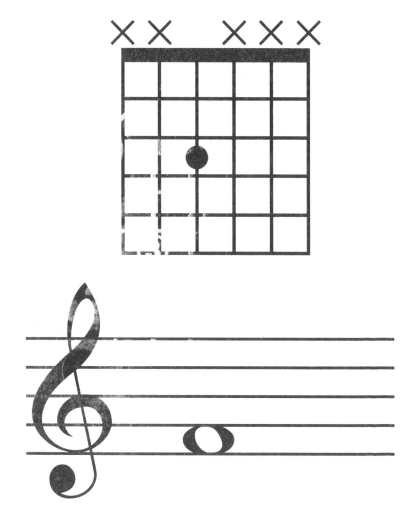

F#

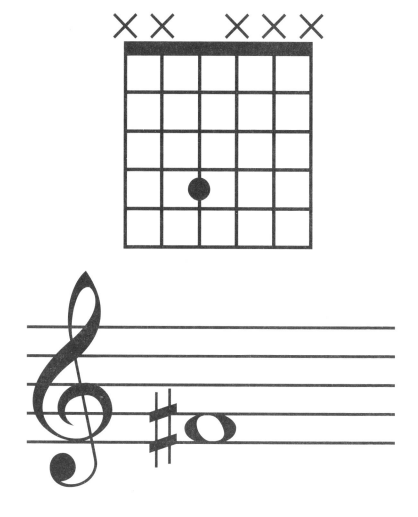

G

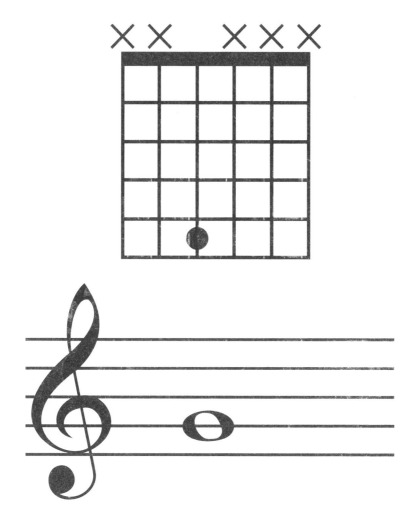

B♭

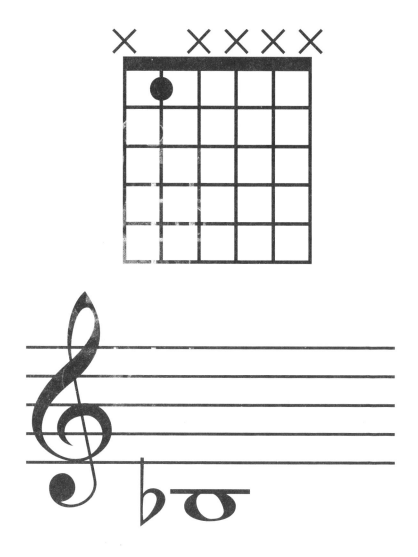

B

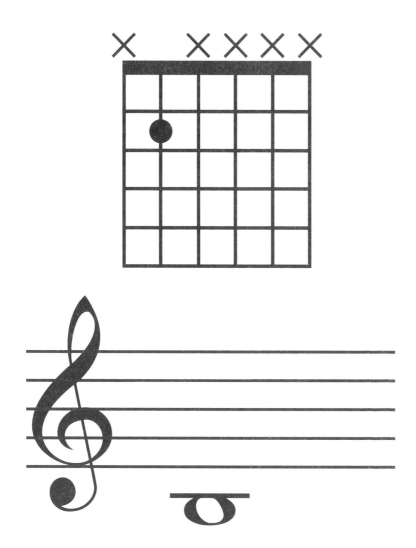

C

C#

D

E

F

F#

G

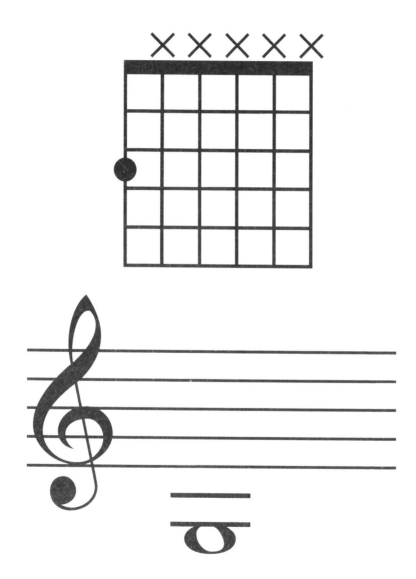

G#

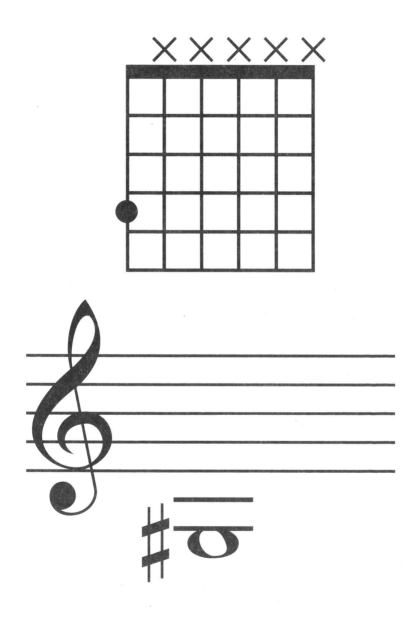

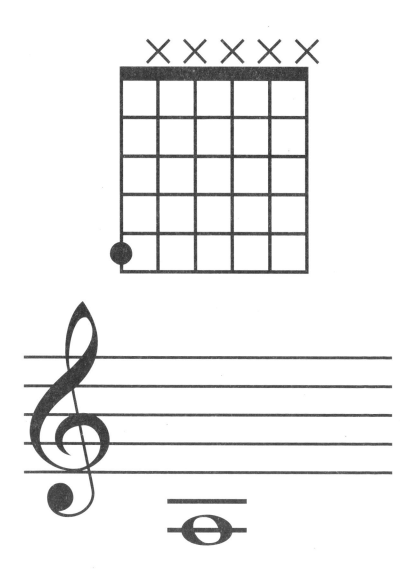

C major
A minor

G major
E minor

D major
B minor

A major
F♯ minor

E major
C♯ minor

F major
D minor

B♭ major
G minor

E♭ major
C minor

A♭ major
F minor

major scale

76

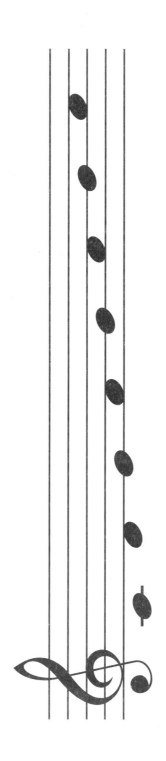

natural minor scale

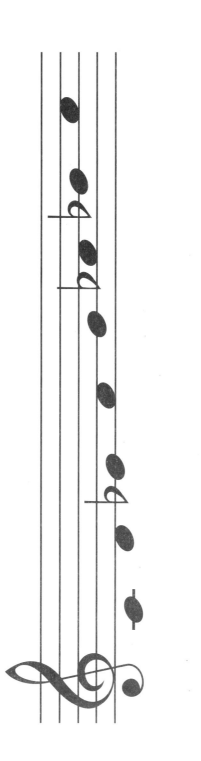

harmonic minor scale

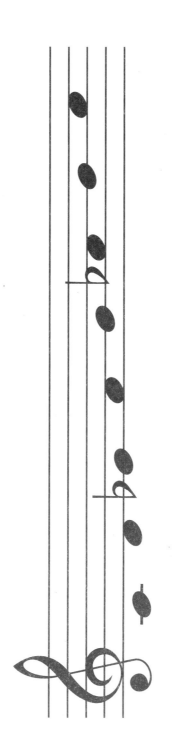

major pentatonic scale

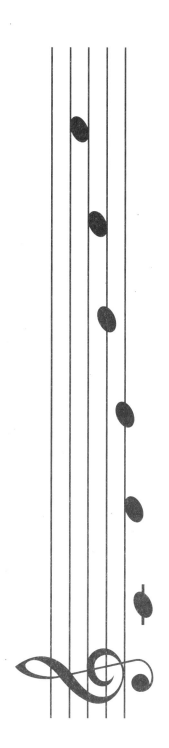

minor pentatonic scale

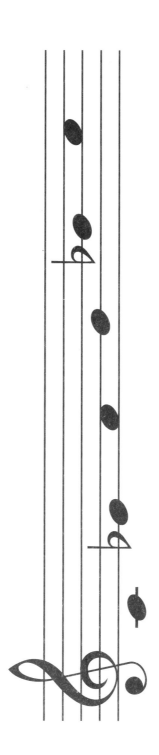

blues scale

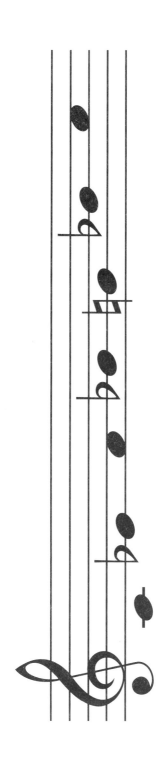

D7

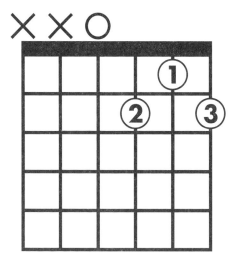

Em

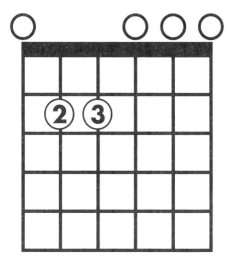

C

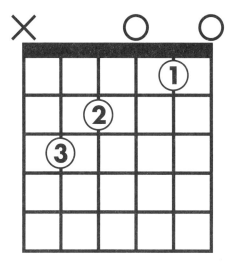

G

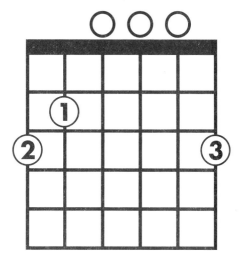

G7

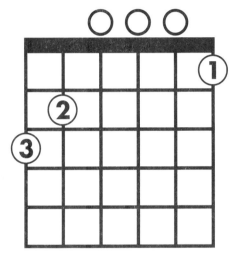

D

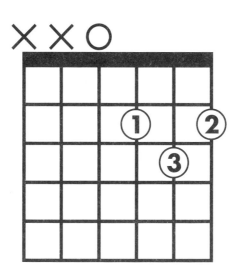

A7

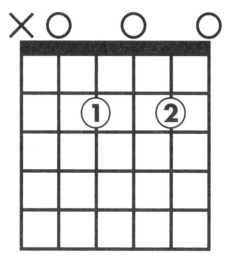

Am

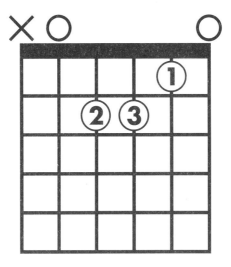

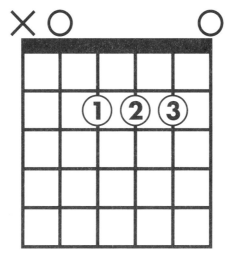

Dm

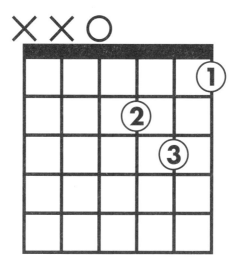

E

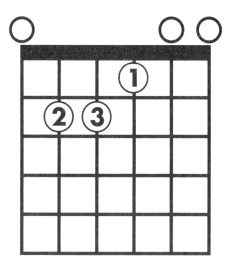

B7

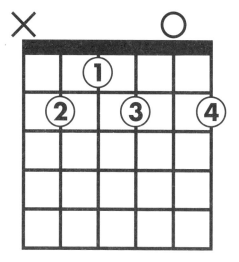

E7

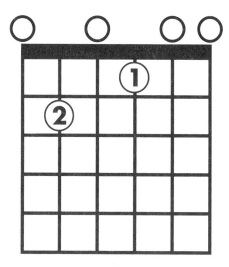

F

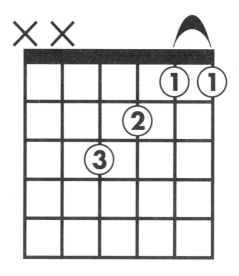

F

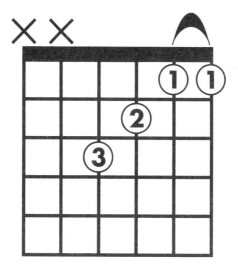

C7

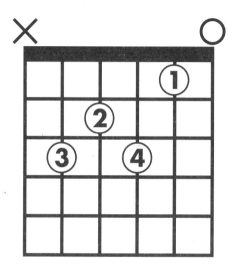